The Future of Ministry

Ministry

Looking Ahead 25 Years

Edited by

Gavin Wakefield

Deputy Warden, Cranmer Hall, Durham

Contributors
Steven Croft
Rose Hudson-Wilkin
David James
Jayne Ozanne

GROVE BOOKS LIMITED
RIDLEY HALL RD CAMBRIDGE CB3 9HU

Contents

The Cover Illustration is by Peter Ashton

First Impression December 2004
ISSN 0144-171X
ISBN 1 85174 580 7

Gavin Wakefield

Ministry 25 Years On...

1

Since the Grove Pastoral Series started 25 years ago it has sought to provide innovative and well-researched thinking across three strands of pastoral ministry from a base mainly in the Church of England:

- Pastoral care
- Ministerial issues
- Pastoral theology

On reaching our century the editorial group thought it would be instructive and fun to invite a number of people to speculate in the area of ministry, not 25 years ago, or now, but where it might be in another 25 years when booklet 200 might be expected.

Our authors were given the wide-ranging question:

> Given where we are now, where do you hope to see ministry being in 25 years' time?

They were then left free to answer it as they will, with the invitation to be as provocative as they wished, writing in a personal capacity. In the event they have been both thoughtful and provocative, and they have been visionary about the possibilities as well as realistic about some of the shortcomings and difficulties, now and ahead. Common to them is a strong sense that small groups or cells will be important for all Christians, and diversity of ministry will be necessary. The ways they describe that future and the emphases they see as important are themselves diverse and stimulating.

Each piece has been only lightly edited and there is no attempt or intention to provide a coherent 'Grove Pastoral vision' for future ministry! Rather, we hope that these essays will spark your own reflections, make you angry, stir you into action, prompt you to wonder if you could not do better in some way…

Gavin Wakefield, Series Convener 2000–2004

2

Steven Croft

Negotiating Tensions

> **Steven Croft** is Archbishops' Missioner, with a brief to facilitate the implementation of the Mission-shaped Church report. Previously he was Warden of Cranmer Hall from 1996 to 2004 and is well known for his writing on ministry and his initiation of the Emmaus nurture course.

As the first Grove Pastoral Series was launched in 1979 I was completing my degree and preparing to go straight on to theological college.

Now as the series reaches its first century, I find myself in mid-ministry (and having recently enjoyed a half-time sabbatical break). Looking ahead another 25 years takes me, I fear, just past three-score years and ten. God willing, the span will mostly be within my active ministerial life. How might patterns of ministry change and develop through that time?

The one certainty is that the context in which the church is called to worship and serve will be a changing one

Even attempting to answer the question seems hazardous. Patterns and forms of ministry are partly shaped by tradition, partly by the life of the church and partly by what is happening in society. The tradition by and large remains the same (although it may be understood and interpreted better or worse or differently with each generation). The society around us has changed rapidly since 1980 and is likely to continue to change still further in the next generation. Who could have predicted 25 years ago that a computer would be a normal working tool of the clergy by 2004? For those who cannot or do not remember that far back, a computer was something which filled a very large room and was given instructions with punch cards. Who can predict now the continuing effects of technology, of more expensive energy, of climate change, and of spiralling debt on the shape of common life and attitudes to faith? The one certainty is that the context in which the church is called to worship and serve will be a changing one.

That changing context will in turn mean that the church itself is in the process of continual transformation—partly responding to the agenda of a changing world (as we perceive and interpret that agenda) and partly responding to our internal agendas for change. Again, over the last generation we have seen a significant number of developments in church life which have changed the way we shape and exercise ministry including the ordination of women as deacons and priests and the owning of more collaborative styles of ministry (or at the very least paying lip service to the ideal).

Alongside these and other developments has been the gradual development over the whole of the last 25 years of a much more missional self-consciousness on the part of the Christian community in the United Kingdom, even within the Church of England. Over the last decade this has come to replace in the churches' thinking, if not yet in its habits and deeper structures, the old Christendom self-consciousness and identity. Mission has rightly become a primary category in our thinking about God and church and ministry rather than a small subsection of pastoral studies. It is this missionary self-consciousness and orientation which needs to be our starting point in creatively imagining how ministry might develop over the next three decades. We understand God as a God who loves and reaches out to the whole of creation. We understand that at the heart of our own calling we are to love God and to love our neighbour. In loving our neighbour we are sharing in God's mission to the world.

The would-be visionary might take some comfort from the truth that all three of these developments in the life of the church were foreseeable and predictable in 1979. Less predictable perhaps was the continuing and accelerating decline in church attendance and most forms of church membership. Over the last two decades we have seen the rise and fall of many individual and simplistic solutions to this overall decline. Out of this experience we have learned at least some lessons. As a church we now no longer believe (on the whole) that things can be reversed if only we all pray for revival, or if only we focus on evangelism, or if only we reshape the liturgy, or if only we all use the same evangelistic programmes (even if that programme is *Emmaus*!). We are perhaps a little wiser, perhaps more conscious of our own weakness, perhaps more aware of the complexity of the problem, and in all this there is hope.

So how might ministry develop in the next 25 years given this new missionary self-consciousness and a starting point of God's grace and love for creation? I offer three tensions to be negotiated rather than simple directions or a pattern. Where ministry is in 25 years' time will depend, I suspect, on how we negotiate these points of tension.

Where ministry is in 25 years' time will depend, I suspect, on how we negotiate these points of tension

Despair and Hope

As a church and as ministers of the gospel, we are likely to be increasingly confronted over the next 25 years with evidence that we are marginal to the life of our society. For individuals and communities the way we view this reality needs to be approached with care lest it breed despair. Great hope and energy were invested in certain sections of the church in the 1990s both in the Decade of Evangelism and (in the charismatic movement) in hope of imminent revival. The decade was fruitful but not in such a way as to reverse the trends of decline in church attendance. The prayers of many for revival were not answered in any obvious ways. A number of publications have identified a lingering sense of disappointment that our best energies did not find a more creative way forward. Where disappointment is not countered it can easily tip into despair. Inevitably, despair affects ministry, sapping energy and undermining faith. Without faith and energy we lack the confidence to preach the gospel with boldness and with the conviction that lives will be transformed. If we are not careful, despair becomes a self-fulfilling prophecy that the future of the church will be barren.

If we are not careful, despair becomes a self-fulfilling prophecy that the future of the church will be barren

We need to remind one another that ours is a difficult context in which to live as a Christian and in which to exercise Christian ministry. All too often, the narrative of decline in church attendance is used to construct a narrative of failure on the part of ministers and ministry. Normally this is done in order to urge change in one particular direction or another to suit the narrator's previous convictions. The by-product is the building of a culture of self-blame on the part of the clergy for the decline in the life of the church. But suppose (as it seems) the church has actually been very well served by its ministers over the last generation. Suppose that, had they not served so faithfully and counterculturally, the church in the UK might be much weaker than it is? Suppose the Lord, in grace and wisdom, wants to affirm all the energy and love and commitment which has gone into sustaining Christian faith in these lands?

If these are difficult and rapidly changing circumstances, then God's people have been here before. In the stories of exodus and exile, in the accounts of the early church and throughout Christian history there are examples and resources for Christian ministers today when it seems that, on the larger scale, all is not well. They are in such times to dig deep into the tradition and in particular to focus on the goodness and the grace and the faithfulness of God. They are also to focus on the encouragement which is to be found in the small and the local: the new initiative which prospers; the lives transformed through an *Alpha* course; the after-school initiative which prospers unexpectedly; the three candidates for adult confirmation. We will need to remind one another of the love and goodness and patience of God and to tell stories of hope to banish despair in difficult times and to encourage (put courage into) one another.

Diversity and Simplicity

The last generation has been one of diversity in recognized ministries. In 1980, the only ordinands in training were male and under 45 with the majority in the age band 26–36. Women were of course training in some of the colleges for recognized lay ministries. In 2004, about half the ordinands in training are female. The age range of those in training will be much wider. Within recent memory in Cranmer Hall we have always had students in training over 55 years of age and our oldest candidate was in her late sixties alongside those in mid-life and in their twenties. The ministries for which people are preparing are also more diverse—self-supporting ministry has been recognized for many years, ordained local ministry only for the last decade or so (and then not in every diocese). There has been a generally helpful proliferation of diocesan schemes to prepare Readers and Pastoral Assistants, Evangelists and Youth Workers. Sometimes there is further diversity in training offered at parish level also. This diversity is, on the whole, a sign of life and creativity—a flourishing and releasing of a wider range of people's gifts and abilities in the service of the body of Christ.

The experience of the early years of the church as witnessed in the New Testament is also one of great diversity in recognized ministries. Look for a moment at three very similar passages where the Pauline epistles use the image of the body of Christ. Each emphasizes that ministry is offered in response to the grace of God and in recognition of gifts given to every member. Each passage recognizes the deeper unity which underlies the diversity of ministries. Each draws out a range of different forms and titles for ministry:

> We have gifts that differ according to the grace given to us: prophecy in proportion to faith; ministry in ministering; the teacher, in teaching; the exhorter, in exhortation; the giver, in generosity; the leader, in diligence; the compassionate, in cheerfulness. Romans 12.6–8

> The gifts he gave were that some would be apostles, some prophets, some evangelists, some pastors and teachers, to equip the saints for the work of ministry, for building up the body of Christ, until all of us come to the unity of the faith and of the knowledge of the Son of God, to maturity, to the measure of the stature of the fullness of Christ. Ephesians 4.11–13

> Now you are members of the body of Christ and individually members of it. And God has appointed in the church first apostles, second prophets, third teachers; then deeds of power, then gifts of healing, forms of assistance, forms of leadership, various kinds of tongues.
>
> 1 Corinthians 12.27–29

The Romans passage is not always understood as a list of 'recognized ministries' as in Ephesians and 1 Corinthians but I think it should probably be read in this way:

- 'exhortation' is a term for public teaching and preaching;

- the term for 'ministry' is *diakonia*—already a recognized term for ministry (see Romans 16.1 and Philippians 1.1);

- 'the giver' may refer to the person who offers help to the needy within the community (see Acts 6.1–6; the word means literally one who shares out);

- 'the compassionate' is possibly a reference to one exercising pastoral ministry or acts of mercy on behalf of the community.

What is clear from a comparison of all three lists is that the early church is trying to find categories and ways of describing Christian ministries and that this flourishing of gifts and ministries is a sign of the work and activity of the Spirit.

However, if we read on in the story of the development of ministry in the New Testament and beyond, the early church could only live with diversity to a certain degree. There came a time when it was necessary also to consolidate and to seek simplicity in the recognition of ministries within the body of Christ. By very early in the second century, the terms used are settling down to the three groups:

- **diaconal** ministries (service of the poor within and beyond the congregation and those exercising ministry which engages with the wider society);

- **presbyteral** ministry (the bifocal ministry of word and sacrament exercised mainly within the Christian community);

- and *episcope* (leadership and oversight of the people of God and of other ministers).

In the last ten years, there has been a renewed exploration of these terms and traditions in the life of the church down the ages. They are helpful because they differentiate not by the gifts of the ministers (as in the earlier lists) but the particular sphere of ministry in which those gifts are to be exercised (society at large, the life of the local Christian community, and oversight of the whole in connection with the wider and historic church). Christian ministry is not representative of the ministry of Christ or of the body of Christ unless it is exercised within these three spheres.

The temptation for a church in a difficult context is to focus on ministry within the life of the Christian community

Over the next 25 years, I hope that emerging and developing ministries would be able to accommodate diversity as the Spirit brings new life but also cherish and nurture simplicity of understanding around the three dimensions of *diakonia*, presbyteral ministry and *episcope*. The temptation for a church in a difficult context is to focus on ministry within the life of the Christian community and on the skills for gathering that community (presbyteral ministry and part of *episcope*). In such a context, we need to ensure there is space and recognition for *diakonia* in all its forms—the ministry and service of the people of God in the world.

Depth and Accessibility

The final (and brief) pairing is the kind of tension which must be resolved through a 'both-and.' If ministers in the coming 25 years are to be effective in serving both church and society, we will need to take care that we are people who are growing both in our depth of understanding and spirituality and knowledge of God and in our ability to make that understanding accessible both within the life of the churches and beyond it.

This must lead in my view to a progressive and steady re-gearing of the life of many Christian ministers. Ministry at its worst over the last 25 years has tended to be activist and somewhat shallow. Far too many people have had an initial period of training and formation which has been followed up by almost no continuing ministerial education or (after the first few years) support or supervision. As time goes by, more and more

As time goes by, more and more is being done with less and less resources and depth of engagement

is being done with less and less resources and depth of engagement. Not surprisingly, it is less effective in an increasingly difficult environment. I believe these ratios and habits need to be profoundly challenged in two ways. In the first place we need to develop much healthier ratios of support and supervision for ministry exercised by both lay and ordained ministers. This means challenging deep seated notions of self-sufficiency and how much can be achieved in a part-time or full-time ministry. In the second place we need urgently to recover and develop a much deeper understanding of the importance of ongoing training and reflection. Depth and accessibility are not opposites but the fruit of real engagement and reflection.

Where do I hope to see ministry in 25 years' time?

- **More hopeful and less despairing** because it draws encouragement from the grace and love of God and from what is happening on a small scale.

- **Cherishing diversity because of the creative gift of the Spirit** yet also seeking to preserve unity and, in particular, the diaconal dimensions of ministry.

- **Developing and holding a wisdom which is both deep and accessible** through the development in turn of habits of ministry built around good rhythms of prayer, community, leisure and work.

Rose Hudson-Wilkin

Confusion and Hope

3

> **Rose Hudson-Wilkin** is Vicar of the Holy Trinity, Dalston and All Saints, Haggerston, and a member of General Synod and Chair of the Committee for Minority Ethnic Anglican Concerns (CMEAC) and of the SPCK board. Married and mother of three children, she enjoys scrabble, travel, reading and entertaining.

The thoughts I am about to share with you on where I see ministry in 25 years are exactly that—my thoughts.

These thoughts are from my experience of being in full-time ministry for over 20 years. I grew up in Montego Bay, Jamaica in what was then known as 'the Church of England' in Jamaica (that is until one of our bishops pointed out how ridiculous it was for the church to be known as the C of E). Thereafter it became the Anglican/Episcopal Church in the Diocese of Jamaica (with diocesan synod approval of course; after all, this is the Anglican Church!). While growing up I watched with interest as the church and its leaders tried to minister with very few resources (leadership, books and finance), at the time thinking this was the norm. In spite of the lack of resources, the churches grew. At one time Jamaica was even renowned for the number of churches per square mile. My local church attracted many young people and, as I write this, I am getting ready to join many of those who shared my Sunday School class for a reunion in New York. I look back on that period with a sense of nostalgia. Here in Britain where I have resided for the last 20 years, I am yet to see the same sense of belonging or the desire to meet up again with others with whom you once learned Bible stories all those years ago.

Here in Britain I am yet to see the same sense of belonging

In order to do justice to the question posed in the opening chapter as I share my reflections on the future of ministry I also need to look at where I perceive it to be at present. I have ministered in the last 19 years in Britain serving in three different dioceses. Between these dioceses there have been innumerable resources—buildings, people, access to literature and to some extent funds— yet the church has continued to struggle to meet the needs of those who come through its doors. I believe this to be so for the following reasons.

1   *The church has been overly possessive.*
    An example of this possessiveness can be seen when the church
    fails to welcome and receive others into its fold. Others are denied
    a place in the house of God because they are labelled as black,
    women, gay, disabled, evangelical, high church—the list goes on.

2   *Within our inner cities where our churches are predominantly black,
    the church fails truly to engage with its black membership.*
    As a result of this there are very few black and minority ethnic
    members in the leadership of the church.

3   *Some of the leadership have not always been faithful ministers of
    the word and sacrament.*
    This may sound like a harsh statement to make. However, as I talk
    with ordinary members of the church, their experience of those in
    leadership has not always been positive. I have often heard clergy
    refer to those in their care as if they are a nuisance. One parishioner
    tells the story of the priest telling her that 'no priest will want to
    come to this parish if they want a successful career.' I ask myself
    with disbelief—where in the Ordinal does it talk about success?

4   *The church has been caught up with the letter of the law rather than
    the spirit of the law.*
    Faculties, listed buildings, huge fundraising targets (to name but
    a few) have found many clergy attempting to swim out of their
    depth.

5   *The church has allowed itself to be caught up in single issue debates.*
    This has been quite destructive—certainly not inspiring 'lost souls'
    to want to come in. Some of these issues that the church is talking
    about are just not where 'the people' are. But we are too busy 'stak-
    ing' our claims.

6   *And last, but certainly not least, as a church we have failed to love
    those placed into our care.*
    Second to preaching the gospel, those who worship in our congre-
    gations need to know that they are genuinely loved and cared for
    within the Christian family—loved enough that their names will
    be learnt, cared about enough to know that when they are missing,
    they will be visited or enquired after, loved enough that time will
    be given to attending, when invited, the various significant events
    in their lives. It is not enough to perform the ceremony (baptism,
    marriage and funeral); it will be important to give time to the social

mingling afterwards, even if it means that the paperwork piles up even further. I listened to one elderly man tell the story of going to a church for approximately six months. He left after that, however, because the priest never learnt his name. He said, 'I knew then that this was not the right place for me.' In one of my congregations we started with twelve to fifteen people. Six left as they were unhappy with having a black (and a) female priest. The congregation has since grown to over eighty worshipping members, with many other visitors turning up from time to time. Time and time again, newcomers refer to the 'warmth they feel within the fellowship' and comment on 'how good it is to hear the Word preached.'

Presently within the church, there is much discussion and debate surrounding what is being called a 'new way of being church.' I would like to contribute to this debate in the light of my experience as a parish priest ministering in inner-city London. For me the words from Ecclesiastes come into their own: 'There is nothing new under the sun.' The 'fresh expressions of church' being shared are not new. They have been going on for some time now but perhaps are only just being recognized as a valid way forward for the church to live and share the gospel. In all the dioceses that I have worked in, both in this and other provinces, small discipleship groups have always played an important part. These groups may not have always been acknowledged from the top, but they have been found to be good practice in enabling members to grow and become confident in their faith.

A few years ago when I visited my home diocese of Jamaica I was invited to a place of work where a weekly half-hour devotion took place. There was singing, prayer, Bible reading and reflection. This was clearly not meant to take the place of Sunday worship but was another opportunity for folks to learn more about their faith, an opportunity to grow. For years many local churches have struggled, in spite of the various hierarchical mandates, to relate at a realistic level to other Christians at their local level. Growing up I was part of a youth congregation, the Anglican Youth Fellowship (AYF) and the Student Christian Movement (SCM). We did not separate ourselves from the adult congregation, but we had youth Sundays and days at school when we worshipped together. As usual, I believe that the church structurally is always playing catch up, discovering what is already happening.

I believe that the church structurally is always playing catch up, discovering what is already happening

What I am about to share with you is twofold. Firstly, my reflections of where I see ministry in the next 25 years (if there are no changes) and secondly, where I hope ministry will be in the next 25 years if the church listens to the Holy Spirit in its midst. So where will the church be if there are no changes? The church will be doing itself a great disservice if it fails to look again at what it perceives its main task to be. While consciously aware of the diverse church that we belong to, I believe that within that diversity, there is a place for us to recognize what is core (or central) to our life of faith and the message that we share. At present there is a confusion, and it is this confusion that will see us failing to grow as Christians, as effective salt giving taste to the world.

It is a confusion of what our core message is which has allowed us to spend 90% of our energies on issues that can never really be core

It is a confusion of what our core message is which has allowed us to spend 90% of our energies on issues that can never really be core. It is the same confusion which is expressed by members of a local congregation preventing newcomers from being involved, and that also sees diocesan and General Synod members deciding on who should or should not be allowed to be ministers of God's Word and Sacraments. It is the same confusion that sees Christians making media-catching outbursts on the assumption that without their intervention, the church will come to some tragic end. If my memory serves me right, I recall Jesus having a saying about the church 'prevailing' against all the odds.

It is clear to me that in 25 years, the church will still be struggling to find itself if it continues to ask the wrong questions, or worse yet to presume that it knows the answer long before it has asked the question to which the answer is needed. As a church, we will be struggling to be a credible witness to the world if we do not wrestle with what it means to be faithful ministers of the word and sacraments. We will be struggling if we do not welcome the gifts and ministries of minority ethnic members found predominantly in our inner-cities. We will be struggling in 25 years if we do not deal with issues about how our buildings should serve us and how we should be caring for the people placed in our care.

I often think of myself as an optimist and it is in the light of this that I want to say where I *hope* ministry will be in the next 25 years. I hope to see a ministry that is fully complementary. By that I mean a ministry that is male and female, black and white. At our baptism, we are all called to represent Christ. Our church must call a halt to the sanctioning of 'segregation' (dressed up of course as a desire to seek inclusion). We must call a halt to veiled threats of a break away if '*some people*' do not have their own way. I remember the day of my ordination being joyful—I had felt this call since the age of 14 years)—but it was also sad, for the women too old to have that dream realized. There was sadness too for a church that had lost so much, and even today we live with the results of that loss. It is a loss that the church has never really acknowledged and perhaps will never really recover from.

As chair of the Committee for Black Anglican Concerns, I am conscious of the large numbers of minority ethnic people who are members of the Church of England but who very rarely are allowed to play an active part in its life. The church is happy to have us fill its pews but does not see us as leaders, able to make major decisions and nurturers of the faith. Minority ethnic members are not looked to as people with a possible vocation to ministry. The potential for growth within the minority ethnic population is a real one because they are instinctively a deeply religious people with a belief in the 'God of their fathers'—a real Old Testament way of being. They are aware of what God has done for them, and they reach out in thanksgiving to that God. In the Old Testament the prophets were always reminding the people of God's goodness and faithfulness to them. Members of the minority ethnic population within our church are not afraid to tell the story of what God has done for them. If the Church of England tapped into this, we would be the ones with the 'good problem' of how we minister to such large numbers.

The church is happy to see us fill its pews but does not see us as leaders

Others have said that we do not need to think about being a large church, we just need to think about being 'salt' or 'yeast' in the leaven of the world. I do want to say, however, that the whole purpose of salt is to flavour the whole, and of yeast to allow the leaven to grow. We need those coming out of theological training and those already in ministry to be thinking about pastoral care, evangelism and teaching and not how we will get to the next rung on the ladder.

The 'dry bones' spoken of in Ezekiel are not quite dry. 'Son of Man, can these bones live?' Yes, I believe there is hope. God's Spirit will prevail. God seeks to breathe new life into his church. The question is, is the church open to receiving him?

4

David James

Cell Future

David James has been Bishop of Bradford since 2002. He tries to lead the Diocese from the edge but sometimes falls over it. He is passionate about the place of young people in the church of today. He has previously been Bishop of Pontefract and a vicar in Southampton and in Sheffield. Before ordination he taught chemistry in university.

'The Church of England as it now stands no human power can save.'

So wrote Thomas Arnold gloomily in the face of the social changes engulfing society and the ecclesiastical establishment in 1832. The technological, cultural and social changes surging around the church are even greater today, so much so that we feel like crying out with the disciples in the storm-tossed boat, 'Do you not care that we are perishing?'

We feel like crying out with the disciples in the storm-tossed boat, 'Do you not care that we are perishing?'

Predictions are that by 2030 the population will be even more elderly than today, with the birth rate perhaps half that needed to sustain numbers. In some of our conurbations ethnic minorities will have become ethnic majorities. Bio-electronic interfaces will be commonplace and while these will offer unimagined advantages the access to 'private' information will lead to lack of trust in personal encounters—'What will you do with my personal history?' IT will continue to bring the world, real and imagined, into our lap(top)s. The lives of our children or grandchildren will become still more fragmented in their various virtual worlds. The developments we have enjoyed in computer technology over the past 25 years will be matched by those that take place over the next quarter century in genetic engineering, and some aspects of science fiction will become reality as intellect and life expectancy are enhanced and designer babies join our brave new world. The poor we shall always have with us, but perhaps more worrying than the relative material poverty will be the poverty of dignity, the lack of self-worth that blights the way we relate to each other.

Which Death Will the Church Have?

Survival is not an option for the church. She has to die but she can choose the means by which she dies. She can hide her face from all that is going on around and be suffocated by what John Tiller called, ten years on from his report *A Strategy for the Church's Ministry*, 'the dynamic conservation of the Church of England, that phenomenon which enables it to summon up enormous energy to avoid having to change,' or she can die to herself and trust that the God who raised Jesus from the dead will give new life to his body on earth. Jesus told his disciples: 'If any want to become my followers, let them deny themselves and take up their cross *daily* and follow me. For those who want to save their life will lose it, and those who lose their life for my sake will save it' (Luke 9.23–4). John Samuel, Bishop of Faisalabad, has commented that it is easy to die once—but we are called to die daily. Today we hear sermons on this passage applied to us as individuals. But the New Testament church—in its courageous witnessing, in its embracing of Gentile believers, in its care for the needy, in the church of Antioch giving up its best people to go overseas, in the Gentile church's generosity (sometimes) towards the church in Jerusalem—also took up daily dying corporately.

Survival is not an option for the church

Dr Arnold may have been unaware in 1832 of the various signs of new life beginning to emerge, including the Anglo-Catholic revival, home and overseas missionary societies and enormous church planting programmes for the industrial towns. What sort of green shoots are emerging today that suggest what ministry might be like in 25 years' time?

The Future is Cell

Early in my time as a bishop I had a glimpse of the future at Holy Trinity, Brompton. I was attending a day conference on church planting and had chosen a seminar on 'planting a youth congregation.' The speaker was Mark Meardon and he described *Eternity*, the youth church in Bracknell. As a vicar in two very different parishes I had tried to put David Prior's *Sharing Pastoral Care in the Parish* into practice but home groups had always remained secondary to church on Sunday and had never found an evangelistic edge. Here a group of young people seemed to be getting it right. Central to *Eternity* are the regular cell meetings led by young people themselves though resourced by the slightly older leadership. The groups come together for their own worship every other Friday and have occasional discos with live DJs, play

Here is a mission-shaped church reaching the parts sadly missing from most of the church

stations and non-alcoholic bar to which friends are invited. *Eternity* is supported by the deanery and through its schools work makes contact in some way with every 11–16 year old in Bracknell. Here is a mission-shaped church reaching the parts sadly missing from most of the church and creating the disciples who will be shaping the church in 25 years' time.

Eternity is a cell church. It is a network church, benefiting from the strong networks that exist among students. It is a church that embraces the culture of those it seeks to reach. It makes use of the internet. It encourages, trains and affirms indigenous leadership (even when young). It is supported by the rest of the church.

Cell churches will become the mainstay of the Church in England. They will offer within an increasingly fragmented society an opportunity to belong. Michael Moynagh notes how both consumerism (surely the spirit of the age) and support groups draw on our innate need to belong, and the church *can* be ideally placed to respond to this need.

> For community is at the heart of church. When someone joins church, hopefully they join a community where they will be loved, in which they can find a framework for life, which will help them nurture their spirituality and to which they can make a contribution, boosting their self esteem. Church should be superbly placed to meet the longing to belong.

John V Taylor wrote in 1975 that

> in many countries the most vital development in the mission of the church in these days has been the formation of 'little congregations,' house churches, factory cells, student groups and so on, whose members meet not only for discussion but in order to experience the whole life of a witnessing, serving, sacramental fellowship at a deeply intimate level.

Many clergy repeat the mantra 'every member ministry' but there is all too little evidence of it in the public life of our parish churches and such laity involvement in worship as there is appears pseudo-clerical. By contrast, in cell-sized churches theology and practice coincide, faith is contextualized, the spiritually blind are given sight and the inarticulate learn to speak.

Such is the mobility of ideas and indeed of people around the world that we are not dependent only upon returning English missionaries for insights from the world church. The Church in England is itself increasingly multi-racial and multi-cultural and this is good for our health and vitality. The Diocese of London is unusual in the growth in numbers it is currently enjoying. One of the perceived causes of this is the high proportion of people of different ethnic minorities in the capital. Many asylum seekers are also Christians and I believe that by 2030 many British Muslims, who already have a respect for Jesus and a spiritual awareness and who are having great difficulty in relating Islam to life in Britain today, will also be in our churches. Their cultures will have found expression in our liturgies and our hymns far more than now and their presence as leaders in the church will be taken for granted. Just as today we invite doctors, nurses and other professionals to 'come over and help us,' we shall welcome an increasing number of mission partners from countries evangelized from Europe not so long ago—and we shall be suspicious of their enthusiasm.

Cell churches have flourished most easily among young people but they are applicable to networks spanning the age range and they feel safe. They lend themselves to meeting in sports centres, pubs, schools and colleges, places of work as well as people's homes. Some will meet (and meet already) on the internet either via chat room or through the successor to video conferencing, and there will be transcontinental cells of people with the same interest or colleagues in an international company. Many cells will have the lifespan of a damsel fly. The mobility of people, their changing work and family or crypto-family situations, differences that cannot be fully resolved will cause some groups to dissipate and die. But if the experience has generally been one of love and acceptance, of healing and wholeness then people will soon want to join another group or start one from scratch.

Ministry in Cells

I have held back from writing much about ministry until now because so often the ministry, that is the ordained ministry, shapes the church and her worship and mission rather than the reverse, so the priest becomes the church instead of the church being the priest.

This will redraw the map of the church, with far more churches and far fewer buildings

When cells do indeed become the key groupings in the church—and in some areas, particularly rural and inner urban, many congregations are little bigger than cells now—this will completely redraw the map of the church, with far more churches and far fewer buildings. It will have enormous implications for ministry and for ministerial training and priestly formation. Leadership will be lay and it will be voluntary and collaborative. We shall have been forced to ask, as Christian churches elsewhere in the world have already asked:

1 If lay people lead the church (and I believe that the cell is a church albeit at the level of 'two or three gathered in my name') what role is reserved for the clergy?

2 How do we resolve the anomaly of the president of a community who cannot preside at Communion?

We shall certainly be looking for leadership and support in spirituality. This is underlined by the impact of *Eternity*. Young people today are not antagonistic towards spiritual matters—they may be ignorant but they are open. More and more are doing their exploring through their GCSEs and A levels and will continue to do so if we have the enthusiastic teachers to help them. And when the storm of life is raging most of us look for that 'Peace, be still' moment. It is significant that amidst all the freneticism of the 2003 NEAC conference in Blackpool's Winter Gardens it was the Archbishop of York's address 'Stop, Look and Listen' that spoke most sharply to the delegates. He reminded his audience that classical evangelical piety 'was not a time of withdrawal into some privatized world of spiritual comfort…but rather issuing in a passionate fervour for social justice and reform—the proclamation of God's kingdom of righteousness, justice, truth and peace.'

I asked some younger clergy who, God willing, will be in active ministry in 25 years' time, what they thought the church of the future might be like. They were remarkably upbeat and not at all daunted by the current situation. They reflected a church coming out of its ecclesiastical ghetto and beginning to engage with the community, living as well as speaking the Good News. One of them wrote for our discussions:

I long for a church to lead in our society and for us to speak out in healing ways about family, relationships, politics, war, not just nationally, of which I am often proud, but locally in our own communities…I basically just long for God to take hold of us, transform us, and use us powerfully to transform our society…I want God to make us a people absolutely gripped with love and bold and fearless in showing it. I want the church in 25 years to be something easily distinguished from our society, and not just because it is irrelevant or out of date! Either that, or the church to look like society because God has transformed them both.

Bishops exhort new incumbents to 'receive the cure of souls which is both yours and mine.' There will be a pontifical bridge-building role, representing the cell to the wider church and *vice versa*, that will be vital in the future if the cell church is to be part of the one catholic church in practice as well as in theory. Cell churches must be eucharistic communities somehow — otherwise there will be a divorcing of Word from Sacrament to the detriment of both. My initial Anglican traditionalism leads me in the short term to look to ordaining very many more people to local ministry within teams of clergy and laity together. However, in a flexible and rapidly changing society in which cells form and divide and some die to sow seeds elsewhere the stamp of indelibility of orders will rest uneasily. By 2030 lay presidency will be taken for granted.

By 2030 lay presidency will be taken for granted

Cells will associate with the wider church in two particular ways, both already present in primitive form in *Eternity*. First, they will come together with other cells for worship, perhaps monthly. What will be appreciated, even though some of the celebrations will only have a couple of hundred people, is the sense of there being 'a host which none can number' gathered together. Some of the cell groups will be committed to a particular celebration while others will 'do the rounds' among celebrations of a variety of cultural styles. It will be from within these gatherings that the 'call' will go out for a new cell to form that will meet in a particular area or seek to connect with a certain group of people. Some celebrations will sponsor bigger projects in the community. The services will engage all the senses and there will be a feeling of intimacy and involvement even in those celebrations that use traditional liturgy and music and there will be a sense of the numinous even in the most contemporary. Nevertheless attendance at celebrations will be far less in total than in the cells.

Second, cells will be linked to the wider church through the internet. Most members will log on daily to study the Scriptures, pray and share news. Providing good IT resources for cells and celebrations will be a major cost for the church. Even so, a number of cells and celebrations will still draw on para-church materials, some of which are very good both theologically and technically. Among the degree courses popular at church colleges will be 'media studies and applied theology.'

The church in 2030 will not have a strong hierarchical structure. Rather there will be a web of relationships between medium to large and small groups and also some umbrella organizations that hold giant festivals. Each particular thread will be fairly tenuous but overall the web will both provide a strong sense of cohesion and considerable flexibility. This will be particularly important since geographical boundaries will have become virtually redundant. There will be only nine or ten dioceses, each with a team of bishops. They will have bowed to the force of their own teaching and accepted

The church in 2030 will not have a strong hierarchical structure

that if the church at the local level is to be collaborative and share leadership then the overseers also must do so. If the church is to hold together in spite of the fissures caused by the ordination of women to the priesthood and the episcopacy and issues around sexuality and around human cloning, then this must be expressed at the episcopal level. But the moral and spiritual authority of a bishop will be more advisory and even less mandatory than at present. Discussions with the Methodists, who by then will have their own bishops and will be in full communion with the Church of England, and with other denominations will have caused a see (*sic*) change in our thinking.

Christ did not come to earth with the aim of establishing fixed forms of ministry or of dividing the world into a series of hierarchical levels. He came to earth to free men and women from the bonds of evil, so that they could learn to love God and their neighbours as themselves. This must also be the purpose of ministries.

Peter Schmidt, in Jan Kerkhofs (ed), *Europe without Priests* (1995)

Jayne Ozanne

Resisting the Final Occupation 5

For the past six years **Jayne Ozanne** has served as an Appointed Member on the Archbishop's Council for the Church of England, where she advises the Church on many strategic and communication issues. She is currently setting up a new Humanitarian Aid charity (HART) with Baroness Cox, which seeks to serve the 'forgotten people' across the world—especially those suffering in the persecuted church.

Growing up in Guernsey is a dream for any adventurous young child.

There are long sandy beaches to explore, miles of cliffs to roam and hundreds of intriguing stories to be uncovered. Most relate to the period of the German Occupation during the Second World War, which sadly affected every family on the island. Our family, like countless others, lost everything. But I never remember hearing a single story about this. Instead, what I do remember were the tributes to 'The Overcomers'—those who were willing to risk everything they had to take a stand for truth, freedom and justice. One such woman, Marie Ozanne, could be found every day in the High Street wearing her Salvation Army uniform (which was outlawed by the Germans) preaching from her Bible. She was one of the few to complain about the deportation of the three local Jewish girls, as well as writing to

I believe that the West is about to face another occupation

protest about the torture by the authorities of slave workers held on the island. Following a lengthy period in solitary confinement in France, she returned to the island where she was poisoned by the Germans whilst in hospital and died. She was buried without any witnesses, as people were too scared to attend her funeral. Sadly few have heard about her brave and lonely stand, although her courage and faith remain as an inspiration to us all.

Perhaps it is because of my upbringing, or maybe it is because of my more recent work with the persecuted church, but I believe that the West is about to face another occupation. Indeed I would go as far as calling it 'The Final Occupation.' As we move into the 21st century, few can doubt that the Christian values that traditionally underpinned our society have been eroded. We have

In contemplating the question 'Where do I see ministry being in 25 years' time?' my response is quite simply — underground!

been invaded, it seems, by a tide of secularism that has silently but determinedly crept up on us, leaving us feeling aliens in our own culture. The Christian church has increasingly found itself at odds with this occupying force, so much so that in many places the church has taken on all the hallmarks of a wartime Resistance Movement. Therefore, in contemplating the question 'Where do I see ministry being in 25 years' time?' my response is quite simply — underground!

Of course, I cannot say that this is where I *hope* ministry will be in the years to come. It is more that this is my impending sense of reality based on what I see happening here in Europe, and what I believe we are being prepared for as a church. A brief glance at global events confirms that these are increasingly difficult times for Christians. We should not be at all surprised by this — the Bible makes it abundantly clear that 'in the world you will have trouble' (John 16.33), and that this 'trouble' appears to get more acute the further through the book you read! However, looking at the cosiness of some of our church meetings I am not always convinced that we fully understand the sacrificial cost required of a life dedicated to serving Christ.

History has proved that the church grows at its fastest when faced with opposition and persecution — indeed there is also much contemporary evidence that bears this out. I am sure that I cannot be alone in being deeply challenged by the horrific stories of brothers and sisters suffering in places like Nigeria, Sudan, North Korea and China. It is in these repressive and often brutal regimes that I am constantly reminded how people are willing to lay down their very lives for their faith. Only last month I heard of the story of a 14-year-old child martyr who was attacked on a Sunday School camp in the Maluku Islands. Standing firm in front of his friends he repeatedly confessed that he was 'a Soldier of God' before first his left arm then his right arm was severed from his body. On asking his attacker what he wanted, the boy was told 'I don't want to harm you, but because you said "I am a Soldier of God," I am going to kill you!' Six children died in this attack, the eldest being only 15. These stories of extraordinary bravery are not unusual, indeed they are happening around the world in increasing numbers. What is unusual, however, is the fact that our media rarely report them.

So what exactly do I mean by the church's ministry 'going underground'? What is the evidence for this happening, and what are the possible benefits? Can the formal church structure continue to operate in such a form, and if so, how? The following few paragraphs offer some initial thoughts on these matters and should hopefully provoke you to further thought and reflection.

My overriding aim is to urge you to 'watch and pray' so that you too may discern the signs of the times. None of us knows what God intends for his church at this hour in history. However, of one thing we can be certain. As we submit to him and obediently walk the path that he has for us, we can rest assured that he has a purpose that he is working out. The Good News, which we must never forget, is that he has already won the battle!

What Does 'Ministry Underground' Look Like?

Underground or Resistance Movements have various characteristics that are integral to their success. I would highlight three that I think are vital. First, they are united in one common purpose. Secondly, every one of their members is willing to pay the ultimate price, despite their obvious fears, because they believe passionately in what (or whom) they are fighting for. Thirdly, and this is key, they trust one another! Indeed, they choose to trust those they do not even know because they are united in a deep love and respect for one another.

The most successful Resistance Movements are those that run on mutual respect and love rather than on power and fear

Of course, one can always find exceptions to this rule, but it would seem that the most successful Resistance Movements are those that run on mutual respect and love rather than on power and fear.

Perhaps I should take a moment to explain what I actually mean when I talk about a Resistance Movement or an Underground Church. Am I picturing cells with secret passwords and closed meetings? No—not at all! But I am thinking of groups of worshippers who know that it may cost them everything they hold dear—their career, their reputation and their relationships with families and friends—if they are 'found out.' This 'outing' may not necessarily be by a political or military regime. In fact, it is far more likely to be by a subtler means such as the media, the work place or the chattering social classes. Once named and shamed, the guilty would be branded 'fundamentalists,' dangerous militants, people who believe that they are right—and that there is such a thing as truth. It is interesting that a senior cabinet politician has already made this very accusation against evangelicals. What is frightening is that it was done in the name of religious freedom!

The irony is that God's commission to each and every one of us is that we be 'found out.' We should be known for our faith, willing to openly acknowledge the God we serve. The challenge will be when faced with the question 'Are we too with Jesus?' whether we respond as Peter did in the courtyard at Caiaphas' house, or like Stephen in front of the Sanhedrin. Can we too hear the cocks crowing, or are we willing to endure the stone throwing?

What I see is a militant army of believers who reach into every element of today's society

So how can this underground movement exist if its members are intent on being found out? Surely it is primed for self-destruction? I believe that the answer is that Christians will discern when and who to talk to about their faith by listening to the prompting of the Holy Spirit. What I see is a militant army of believers who reach into every element of today's society—touching every level of politics, education, health and business. This army needs no formal structure. Instead it instinctively knows how to 'be church' in whatever setting it is found. It is a formidable army—united by love, strengthened by joy and secure in the knowledge that death has been defeated by the Cross.

Can the Formal Church Structure Continue to Exist?

This is an interesting question. All groups need good leadership—the Bible makes this very clear. However, there is a difference between demanding a 'king' as the Israelites did, and recognizing the God-ordained leader that God has appointed over them. The critical difference here is that the former was originally desired by the people so that they could be seen to be like other nations, whilst the latter was raised up independently by God. The former receives their power and authority through the law of the land, often exerting a certain amount of force to implement it. The latter relies on the love and respect of the people he or she serves, and whilst they have no 'official' power or authority they have great influence. I would define this as having 'moral authority.'

The structure that is most likely to work is one that naturally emerges from the grass root

The structure that is most likely to work in an organization founded on mutual trust and respect is one that naturally emerges from the grass roots. God always raises up leaders, and they are usually recognized by the people they are commissioned to lead—just look at Moses, Joshua and Gideon. This, in a sense, is what is already happening today in the various evangelical movements, where an overarching leadership structure is forming. We also see this in network organizations such as New Wine and Lydia, where people are brought into senior leadership positions independent of whether they are lay or ordained because the people they serve recognize them as God's appointed leaders. So there is a structure of sorts; it is just not one you can pre-empt or plan for. It can only be given to us by God.

Who Will Make Up This Resistance Movement?

One of the most exciting things I see happening in the West today is the growth of a new 'Joshua army' made up primarily of young people who are completely committed to following Jesus. These soldiers of Christ are dedicated, disciplined and determined. Most have already learnt the hard way that following Christ leads to alienation. Yet they also know that there is power in the cross, that the God they serve is a God of love who can and will move mountains if they ask him. These are the early recruits of the Great Resistance Movement. It is they who will make up the core of the Underground Church that will exist in 25 years' time, with many serving as its God-ordained leaders.

They had sold themselves short — believing the best thing to maintain peace was to work with the enemy

The critical question for the rest of us will be whether we have turned tail and become collaborators with the occupying forces, or whether we too will be resistance fighters — underground, ready to pay with our lives for the things that we believe in. It is interesting that many collaborators during the Second World War were often given positions of power and authority. Of course they claimed to have the interests of the people at heart, but they had sold themselves short — believing the best thing to maintain peace was to work with the enemy, rather than taking a stand for the greater cause of freedom, truth and justice. I pray that this might never be said of the church.

How Will This Army minister?

It is of no surprise that the best selling contemporary Christian book of recent years is one devoted to examining the greatest gift that God has given us, and the most powerful weapon that he has placed in our armoury — that of love. I found *What's so Amazing about Grace?* such a powerful book that I decided to give each member of the Archbishops' Council a copy for Christmas one year. I did not expect them all to have time to read it, but I did pray that they would read the first page in which Philip Yancey shares a disturbing story about a young girl in crisis. When asked why she had not thought of coming to the church earlier for help, she exclaimed: 'Church?! Why on earth should I go there?! I was already feeling bad enough about myself!' Why is it, I wonder, that the church has become better known as a place of truth and judgement than for its ministry of grace? Jesus perfectly embodies both — overwhelming us with his love, whilst showing us the way of truth. The church must learn to do the same, proving that in all circumstances love *never* fails.

A Final Thought

In 25 years' time I will be over 60. My prayer is that by then we will have a united, trusting and sacrificial church of whom it will be said:

> And they overcame him by the blood of the Lamb and by the word of their testimony. They did not love their lives so much as to shrink from death.
>
> Revelation 12.11